from various sources. Please consult a licensed professional before attempting any techniques outlined in this book.

By reading this document, the reader agrees that under no circumstances is the author responsible for any losses, direct or indirect, that are incurred as a result of the use of information contained within this document, including, but not limited to, errors, omissions, or inaccuracies.

Table of Contents

Chapter 1: Why Popcorn? 7

Chapter 2: How Will You Make Money? .13

Chapter 3: What You Need to Get Started 25

Chapter 4: How to Get Your Business Poppin' 33

Chapter 5: Scaling and Growing Your Business to Unimaginable Heights 55

Gourmet Popcorn Business

Sell Interesting Flavors of a Classic Snack That Will Have Customers Craving More

Glenn Sarratt

© **Copyright 2024 - All rights reserved**.

The content contained within this book may not be reproduced, duplicated or transmitted without direct written permission from the author or the publisher.

Under no circumstances will any blame or legal responsibility be held against the publisher, or author, for any damages, reparation, or monetary loss due to the information contained within this book, either directly or indirectly.

Legal Notice:

This book is copyright protected. It is only for personal use. You cannot amend, distribute, sell, use, quote or paraphrase any part, or the content within this book, without the consent of the author or publisher.

Disclaimer Notice:

Please note the information contained within this document is for educational and entertainment purposes only. All effort has been executed to present accurate, up to date, reliable, complete information. No warranties of any kind are declared or implied. Readers acknowledge that the author is not engaging in the rendering of legal, financial, medical or professional advice. The content within this book has been derived

Introduction

Popcorn, it's a delicious snack that everyone loves. Seriously, how many people do you know that don't like popcorn? It's a popular snack for watching sporting events or at the movies.

People buy plenty of it at the store to snack on. Nobody can seem to get enough of this food item and that's a good thing for you. Plenty of companies out there are making a nice chunk of change from popcorn, and the cool thing is that you can too.

Even if you're brand new, there are plenty of things that you can do to stand out and have people coming back for more. You probably have a lot of questions and your head might be spinning because you don't even know where to begin. Luckily you can breathe easy because everything will be sorted out after you read this book.

I want to help guide you through the process of knowing what materials you need to get, how to price your popcorn, how to sell your popcorn, and plenty of other things in between. So let's go ahead and get things popping, shall we?

Chapter 1: Why Popcorn?

In this world, there's no shortage of things you can do to make money. So why then should you consider getting into the popcorn business when you have so many other options out there? Well, the following are some of the reasons why I think this business is such a good idea to start:

People Are Trusting of Food and They Know It's Not a Scam

Imagine for a second that you decided to start a used car dealership. People are trusting of cars, but people can be skeptical of buying a used car depending on where they're buying it from. There's the stereotype of the used car salesman in the industry, and in order for you to be successful you're going to have to build that trust with people who have never heard of you before.

That's a tough hill to climb and there's no point in trying if you can just do something else where the trust is built in. Popcorn is one such thing with inherent trust because it's a food item.

Naturally, people know what they're getting with food. So it's not a matter of them trusting the product itself, it's a matter of them trusting a business they've never heard of.

Luckily for you though when people think of a small company that sells popcorn, they tend to think of homemade popcorn that they can't get just anywhere. They know they're going to get something that tastes way better than the popcorn they could buy off the shelf at the grocery store. It comes down to getting enough exposure for your business. Then once people try it, your popcorn has to be good enough for people to come back for more.

Easy to Store and to Ship

With most food-based businesses, things can get complicated quickly. You're going to be dealing with food that needs to be refrigerated and this can complicate things quickly. It can make you change up your entire business model and it's all centered around the fact that you can't easily ship your food out or store it easily.

With popcorn, that isn't a problem you have to worry about. Popcorn doesn't need to be refrigerated, which makes things a lot easier for you to store. Then once it comes time to ship out the popcorn, that will be easy as well since you don't have to worry about keeping the popcorn at a certain temperature or securing it super well as it isn't fragile.

Can be Done from Your Home in Most Cases

One problem with a lot of food companies is that you're unable to operate from your own home. While there's no guarantee that you'll be able to operate from your home as laws vary depending on what state you live in, this typically won't be an issue in most cases. I'm going to talk about cottage food laws later on in another chapter, but for a lot of food companies, operating from home isn't going to fly.

This means you're going to have to get additional space to prepare your food or rent a commercial kitchen time and again to make your food. All of this adds to your operating expenses and initial start-up costs. The goal of any business is making a profit and those costs can make it challenging to get things going. You might not have the extra money to be able to do something like that right away and with a popcorn business, it isn't something you likely have to worry about.

Great Margins

What if I told you that it's not unheard of to make 80% profit margins from the popcorn you sell? It is absolutely a reality depending on pricing and the type of popcorn you're selling. Even if your margins are on the lower end, they'll still be higher than most businesses. The goal for most businesses is a 50% profit margin, but even that is unobtainable in certain industries due to high operating costs. Some businesses such as gyms for example typically make around a 10% profit margin. When you're able to buy something for cheap and make good money from it, that's a sign of a great business opportunity.

Easy to Make

Let's say I told you that you could make great money by starting your own custom bicycle business. Well even if that is true, the process of making a bicycle is complicated. If you know nothing about how to build a bike, then you're going to spend a lot of time just learning the skill itself before you actually get to sell any bikes. With popcorn, you can pop right into profitability because the skill bar is low when it comes to making delicious popcorn.

You Don't Have to Spend a Ton of Money to Get Started

A popcorn business can be started for a relatively cheap amount of money depending on how you approach things. I'm going to cover the supplies you'll need to start a popcorn business soon enough but think of how many people are not able to start a business because of how much money it can cost. When you take a budget-friendly approach to starting a popcorn business, you're not going to be breaking the bank, which is a good thing.

There Are a Ton of Different Varieties that You Can Make

When people think of popcorn, they typically think of buttered popcorn and you can definitely make good money just from the classic popcorn that everyone thinks of. You have other varieties such as kettle corn, cheddar, and caramel. And then there's really any type of creative flavoring that you can think of. These are just a few ideas, but there are countless others:

-Chocolate drizzle
-Ranch
-Buffalo
-Cookies and Cream
-Bar-B-Que
-Jalapeno
-Peanut Butter
-Cinnamon
-Coconut

And of course, you can combine things like chocolate and peanut butter, but there are so many possibilities that you'll never get bored. You can always experiment and try out different things as much as you want! This business does not have to be some monotonous thing where you're constantly doing the same thing over and over.

Chapter 2: How Will You Make Money?

With a popcorn business, there is a good amount of variety in how you can sell your popcorn. This is a business and at the end of the day, it's about making money in the most efficient way possible in the beginning. As time goes on, you can expand your footprint and start doing things that allow you to maximize your profitability.

The Online Shop

The first model for making money from this business happens to be the best way to get started. I would consider it essential for you to have some sort of online presence when it comes to trying to sell your product. Creating an online website where people can place an order is the cheapest and most expansive way to make money.

Once your website is up and running, you can now make a sale from anywhere. You're not limited to just your local area. Getting a website up and running isn't the cheapest thing and there are cheaper ways to try and sell your popcorn.

But nothing is going to give you a wide range of access to new customers quite like a website can. Additionally, in the modern age, people expect companies to have websites. It's a good way to build trust with people who are being exposed to your business for the first time. This is why I believe that having a website is an important step you'll want to take no matter what your long-term goals are for your company.

The Subscription Model

With the subscription model, people will pay a monthly fee and they'll be sent popcorn at a certain interval. Typically this will be in the once-per-month range, but it can be more often than that if you want to. I really like this model a lot because it's guaranteed revenue for your business every month.

You can see a lot of companies trending towards this idea as well. There are lots of streaming services that require a monthly fee. Food companies will send their product on a monthly basis such as their meat or whatever else.

Even video game companies are using this model too where you pay a monthly fee and gain access to a certain library of games. Popcorn is the perfect item to put as a subscription. There are so many ways you can go about it due to the variety of flavors that can be created.

You can have it to where someone is sent a new flavor every time or they're sent the same flavor if they have a particular favorite. When it comes to making money off of a subscription model, you don't want to be stiff with it. Offer people more options than just receiving one bag per month.

Give them some options for how many bags they want to receive per month and how frequently they want to receive them. For example, the customer could choose a weekly, biweekly, or monthly option. Then they could choose the number of bags that they want to receive on each shipment.

So someone could choose to receive 2 bags every two weeks for example. You could even offer discounts per bag the more bags someone signs up for. Offering a better price is an important factor to consider.

If someone can just buy a bag when it's convenient for them to do so at the same price as a subscription, then why should they sign up? You need to offer an incentive for people. You could offer their first bag for 50% off and then each subsequent bag is 10% off from the normal price. Front loading the initial offer with a big discount helps to push people to sign up and then the smaller discount will help them stick around.

Allowing people to easily cancel at any time is important as well. Charging less than normal isn't fun, but remember you're going to have high margins from this business. It's okay to sacrifice a bit of that margin in exchange for the predictable recurring revenue that you'll be generating from your subscription customers every month.

Lastly, it's worth noting that you don't want to only offer subscriptions. Oftentimes people will want to try your product first before committing to it with a subscription. Having a subscription model in addition to one-off sales is the perfect combination.

Sell at a Stand or Event

I'm sure you've seen people selling their produce on the side of the road before. And if you've ever gone to a flea market before, I know you've seen people selling popcorn and other food items for people to eat while they walk around and shop. These methods are some cheap ways to start getting your product directly in front of people.

I wouldn't recommend these as being your sole way of making money though. Having an online presence is more important to establish first. I would view this as something you should do as a supplemental thing to your online store.

The thing I like about this is that it gives you an avenue to test the waters if you're considering opening a physical store. You can test out various signage and offers and see what gets people to buy and what doesn't. Though not exact, it gives you an idea of what it's like to sell in person where you're going to be relying on foot traffic and catching people's attention to sell more popcorn.

Starting with a flea market, food market, or food trade show is a good idea because these events will draw a crowd. You don't have to worry about location or getting people to come because all of this will be taken care of for you. With a stand on the side of the road, you have to look into getting a permit from your city.

Your location also matters a lot. One spot could be a total flop while another could be worth your time. The best way to go about something like this is to mix it in when you can. It's a good way to help expand your customer base and help with word of mouth as time goes on.

The benefit of selling in person is that you can offer free samples to let people try your product on the spot. This will work as an instant trust builder and get people hooked on your product. When people are buying online, skepticism will be higher than in person because there's no way for someone to be able to try before they buy.

Brick and Mortar

The last option for how you can make money with this business is by opening a store with a physical location. This by far will be the most expensive way to operate your business, but it will give you some benefits. You'll have a location where you can make your popcorn, store it, and sell it. And as long as the location is good, it will serve as a continuous advertisement for anyone who passes by.

This essentially acts as another method for you to make money in addition to other efforts such as your online store. The downside though is that the costs to get your own building are going to be pretty high. Not to mention the equipment you'll need and paying the lease every month. If you're on a budget this isn't going to be a feasible option to start with. It's something that makes more sense down the line as you start looking to expand your business.

Will You Offer Delivery or Ship No Matter What?

Another factor you need to consider is what you'll do for local orders if your main presence is online. You could offer to have the customer come to you and pick up their order, you could take it to them, or you could ship it to them. Shipping or delivering will cost you money, but customer pickup will save you time and money.

This can be seen as an inconvenience for the customer though, so it's not necessarily a good option unless the customer suggests the idea themselves. For the sake of time, I recommend shipping to your customers even if they are local.

Trying to add in delivery adds a whole logistics layer to your operation. By shipping in any scenario, you help to keep things as simple as possible. It will allow you to put more time into marketing, trying out new recipes, or serving your other customers.

What Should You Charge?

Ultimately, you can determine what you think is right when it comes to pricing. You could come up with some unique ideas that have a higher cost to make and therefore you need to charge more. I do want to provide you with some general advice when it comes to pricing.

If you're not sure what to charge a good place to start is $9.99 for a 12-ounce bag of popcorn. I would start with this price point if you're selling regular buttered popcorn. For any type of specialty popcorn that you're selling, a good place to start would be $12.99 for a 12-ounce bag.

It's also important to note that these prices don't include shipping costs. So whenever your customer makes the purchase, the shipping cost will be added to the price point. If you want to offer free shipping for your customers, then you'll need to adjust your prices to help offset this expense.

Doing this isn't a bad strategy as a lot of customers have come to expect free delivery from online purchases that they make. The good news about pricing is that it's dynamic. You don't want to come up with an initial price point where you start and stick with that for the entirety of your business's life.

Inflation and operating costs alone will force you to increase your prices over time anyway. So the best thing you can do is not be afraid to be fluid with your pricing. It's a scary thing to increase your prices because we don't want to lose customers. But if you make small incremental changes and wait to see what happens before you up them again, then most of your customers won't care as long as your popcorn is good.

What is Your Unique Selling Proposition?

Some businesses are extremely unique and you don't have to worry about standing out because inherently nobody is doing what you are. When it comes to popcorn though, there are plenty of other people and companies trying to get their slice of the popcorn pie. Your unique selling proposition is the thing that makes your business unique. It's the thing you can point to that no one else can.

You can continue to use your unique selling proposition to sell more popcorn over and over again. So you really have to ask yourself, why should someone buy popcorn from you instead of from someone else or the store? If your popcorn is more expensive than something someone can buy at the store, then it better taste a lot better.

Otherwise, why should someone buy what you're offering? In order to properly determine what your unique selling proposition is you need to do some research on your competition. See what they're offering. Do they have unique flavors?

If so, how many different flavors do they have? Are they competitive on price or do they offer free shipping or even express shipping for free? You need to gather some intel about the kind of offerings that your competitors have.

This will allow you to know what you can do to help you stand apart from them. The other place you want to do research is with the customers themselves. This of course can't happen until you gain some customers.

Once some people do start buying from you, it's important to send an email, text, or some other form of communication with them. You want to ask what made them want to buy from you. This will help to give you valuable insight directly from the people that matter most.

This can then allow you to change your selling proposition if need be if you discover that people are consistently buying for one reason or another. Maybe you need to offer some unique flavors that no one else has. Maybe you need to offer free shipping if no one has done that.

Create a unique purchasing option such as a sampler pack so multiple flavors can be tried out at once. There are lots of ways that you can separate yourself from anyone else in this space.

Once you have come up with a unique selling proposition, you want to bring it up time and time again whenever you're marketing your company.

Mention it on your social media posts, in ads, on your website, and wherever else. You want to make it known that you offer something that people can't get anywhere else. For example, if you're the only popcorn business that offers a unique flavor, then people are going to have to come to you for that flavor.

Now just having that flavor isn't going to do anything for you, you have to make the most of it. Feature that flavor in as many different ways as you can. Mention how it's your most popular flavor or how most repeat customers come back for this flavor. Do whatever you can to get people to try that flavor because if they like it, they have to come back to you for it no matter what.

Even as time goes on and you might have to increase your prices, people can't leave and go somewhere else because there is nowhere to go. That's the power of having a unique selling proposition.

Chapter 3: What You Need to Get Started

As I talked about earlier in this book, one of the great things about a popcorn business is that it doesn't require a lot of supplies or money in order to get started with it. There are of course some things you'll need to purchase and there are some additional things you'll need to take care of to officially get your business up and running.

Food Supplies You'll Need for Popcorn

When it comes to making basic popcorn, you really don't need that much. All you really need are popcorn kernels and vegetable or coconut oil. This is all you need food-wise to create basic popcorn. However, this popcorn would be pretty bland and it wouldn't be wise for you to expect people to come back.

Other necessities such as butter and salt will help to spice things up a bit and allow you to be able to make a staple which is buttered popcorn. More than likely though, you won't want to stop there. You'll want to buy any other food supplies to make unique flavors that you'll want to sell. This might include cinnamon, bar-b-Que sauce, jalapeños, or whatever else it is that you're able to come up with.

A Popcorn Machine

You'll need a way for your popcorn to actually pop and there's a wide range of machines that you can buy. They vary in terms of price greatly. On the low end, you could be paying $50 or up to $10,000 on the high end.

In the beginning, going all out on a machine is certainly overkill. You likely won't have the space for it and it will produce way more popcorn than you'll need. A $50 machine might suffice.

It will be compact enough for you to easily be able to utilize wherever you're operating from. The only thing you'll have to worry about is the amount of popcorn that it can produce. In the beginning, this probably won't be an issue, but you can outgrow it rather quickly.

So it is possible to skip a cheaper machine and go for something more mid-range that's in the $250-$300 range. Surprisingly enough, many major retailers will sell popcorn machines that will more than suffice to help get your feet off of the ground. The main question is if you want to start with something more basic in the $50-$75 range or something in the $250-300 range.

The main difference comes down to the amount of popcorn that you'll be able to produce. The last thing you want to run into is not being able to make enough popcorn to be able to keep up with your orders. However, in the beginning, this likely won't be an issue. This is why I recommend starting out with a smaller machine.

This will help you save on your initial start-up costs. It also gives you a chance to test the waters and see how you like things. The machine itself won't take up very much space either. Then once you're ready to upgrade, you can then sell your old machine to help cover a little bit of the cost for the new one.

Plastic Bags

You're going to need a way to store and ship your popcorn and this is the obvious way to go about doing that. You can buy plastic bags in various sizes depending on what kind of offerings you want to have. For instance, you could buy 6-oz bags, 12-oz bags, and 18-ounce bags so that you can offer different sizes to your customers.

The last thing you'll need are boxes for shipping out your product, but aside from that, that's all you really need to get started with this business. The list is pretty short, right? While that may be it from a product standpoint, there are some other things that you'll need to get your business up and running.

Are you Allowed to Sell Popcorn from Your Own Home?

Something you're going to want to determine before starting is if you'll be allowed to make and sell popcorn from your own home. Each state has varying laws on what you can and can not sell from your home regarding food items. These are known as cottage food laws.

Generally speaking, some states will allow you to operate from your home kitchen so long as your annual sales don't surpass a certain amount and the foods that you're selling don't require refrigeration. You'll need to look up cottage food laws for the state that you're currently residing in and see what the particulars are for your state. You may also need to get a food handler's permit, business license, and sales tax permit in addition to other things.

To learn the specifics of what's needed for your area, it's best to contact the health department and government officials in your county. Of course, if you are selling online and shipping to other states, then different laws and regulations may be in play, so it's best to consult with an attorney to make sure your business complies with all laws and regulations.

Business Insurance and LLC

I also recommend that you get in contact with an insurance agent and discuss a policy that makes the most sense for your business needs. In most cases, this is going to be a general liability policy that will help to protect you against a wide range of events that could happen as a result of operating a food-based business. The other thing I would look into doing is forming an LLC.

This is a business structure that's perfect for a small business when starting. Something such as a C corporation is likely unnecessary as it's intended for companies that eventually want to go from a private company to a public company one day. This of course will allow the company to sell shares to the public and make a lot of money doing so, but there are some major trade-offs such as double taxation.

You might be thinking why even form an entity at all? Why not just stay as a sole proprietorship? Well, this is your business so ultimately you get to decide what you want to do. The cool thing about an LLC is that your popcorn business will become its own entity.

Instead of you and your business being viewed as one and the same, as is the case with a sole proprietorship, your company will take on a life of its own. This will help to keep your personal assets separate from business assets. This is a critical distinction because in the event of legal action, your personal assets will be out of the picture.

Practice Makes Perfect Popcorn

One other thing you need to think about before you start putting your popcorn out into the world is to start practicing. With this business, it's important to have a good handle on your recipe before you start shipping your popcorn out to customers across the country. You don't have to be a perfectionist and have something groundbreaking, but you'll want to make sure that you're able to consistently produce good popcorn time after time.

Most entrepreneurs will not agree with this premise. Business is about sales, after all, so some will recommend that you start selling before you're ready. This way you'll be able to get some cash flow and help to pay for your expenses along the way.

When it comes to a food business, I don't think this is the right approach. Your first customers are very important to your success for multiple reasons. They can help to get the word-of-mouth snowball started.

They can also make or break your confidence with a review. Let's say you get an order and then you start scrambling to get things together such as your supplies. Now you're also scrambling to try and put together the perfect popcorn recipe.

You're going to be doing all of this and what if the customer doesn't like it and they leave you a bad review? Imagine what that will do to your confidence. It can absolutely be crushing and it will just make it that much harder for you to make sales going forward. So instead it's okay to have some patience to be able to craft a recipe that you will be confident with.

Once you reach that point, then you can start to market to the general public to start bringing in sales. From there you can start to tweak and perfect things and add in additional flavors. Also if you're not sure if your popcorn is good or not, gather up some friends and have them do a taste testing.

Make sure you use friends that will be honest with you. If someone is being nice and they only say positive things even if the popcorn is completely burnt, for example, that isn't doing you any favors. You need honest feedback so you can improve your product. You could even do a blind taste test and put your popcorn up against store-bought popcorn to see what your friends prefer more.

Chapter 4: How to Get Your Business Poppin'

Once you feel confident with a popcorn product that you want to bring to the public, it's now time to start marketing your business so that you can start to acquire some new customers. This is a crucial component of your success. You may very well have the best popcorn this planet has to offer, but that doesn't guarantee success. In fact, someone who has a sharp marketing skill set will still make more money than you even if they have a subpar product.

This is all due to the fact that people will actually know the marketing genius's product exists. People can't buy your popcorn if they don't know about it. Let that sink in for a second. People will spend their money on worse popcorn simply because they know about it, and they won't buy from you if you don't market correctly.

The trouble with marketing is that there are endless ways and possibilities for which you could promote your business. Some of them cost money and others will be more time intensive. No matter what strategy you employ, it will work to a certain degree. The question is how much effort did you have to put in and how much exposure did it give you? You could spend hours designing the perfect flyer, but if you put those flyers in a dead part of town, nobody will see them.

Even if you put them in an area where they will be seen, if it doesn't convert to sales, then it doesn't matter. You just wasted your time when you could've been employing a different marketing strategy. In this chapter, I want to share with you the things that will yield the highest return on your investment.

Do a Pre Launch to Build Hype

Yet another reason why it makes sense to practice your popcorn recipe before you sell is so that you can make the most of your pre-launch. A pre-launch is an amazing idea for any new business that's about to officially open. Sadly though many new companies fail to take advantage of this. Some will do a fantastic job of this. One such example is when a new fast food restaurant opens up and they offer the first customer free burgers for a year. Or they'll offer the first 100 customers some type of reward.

On the surface, doing something like this may seem expensive to pull off so why even bother, but that couldn't be further from the truth. People will wait outside for days to be the first customer. This alone gets people talking. Then for the customer that gets the free food, it's unlikely that they'll come by every day and even when they do, they'll likely buy something else along with it so the restaurant is still making money.

But the hype and word of mouth that this creates helps to drive a huge amount of customers in the beginning days. This can then help to snowball word-of-mouth marketing. So how can you take advantage of this with your popcorn business? Well if you're operating from home and predominantly selling your popcorn online, you can use the internet to your advantage. The thing is you likely already have personal social media accounts with your friends and family following you. This is a great place to start to lay the foundation for your customers.

The reason is that these people already know and trust you, so they're going to be more open to the idea of purchasing popcorn from you. Then from there if your popcorn is really good, they're going to spread the news and tell their friends, which can really help to get the ball rolling. So most of your pre-launch strategy needs to involve a series of posts on your personal social media pages leading up to the day of your launch. Even though you're going to be creating some business profiles, your new accounts won't have enough followers yet for this strategy to make a difference.

To make this effective you need to allow some time to let the hype build up but not too long to where people lose interest. The optimal amount of time for this is about 1-2 weeks in most cases. Here's the first type of post that you should make when you're ready to announce that you're going to be starting a business:

"Hey everyone! One of my favorite foods of all time has always been popcorn. I of course love eating popcorn when I watch movies or just as a delicious snack. There are so many reasons to enjoy popcorn. The thing is I often find myself craving something better. Something unique that you can't just get at any store. So one day I was eating a commonly known food and thought to myself, you know what this doesn't sound half bad with some popcorn! So I experimented and created a flavor that I believe is equally unique as it is flavorful. Stay tuned for my next series of posts where I'll share more about what this unique flavor is!"

What I like about this post is that you're giving a backstory for why you're starting the business. Your story will likely be different from this, but you can use this as a guideline for pre-launching your business. The backstory and love for popcorn give a reason for why you're starting this business. It wasn't just on a whim that you decided to start this business. That wouldn't land as well with people because it makes it feel more like you're just doing it for the money.

Then you're also ending the post on a cliffhanger. People are going to be more likely to keep up with your next post because they're going to be curious as to what the flavor is going to be. You don't have to use a unique flavor as your hook, but you do need to come up with something intriguing that will have people coming back. I would wait a day or two and then post my next post.

I would give a brief overview of the previous post and then ask people what they think the unique flavor is. If you're posting this on your story, you can have people vote on a poll. If you're posting on your feed, then you can ask people to leave a comment with what they think the answer is.

You can even get the best of both worlds by posting on your story and on your feed. Then once you post this I would again wait a couple of days and make a post sharing the answer. I would end the post by teasing that you're going to share a special offer in your next post so stay tuned.

After waiting another couple of days, I would share the offer. Mention how your popcorn will be discounted for a limited time such as the first 48 hours that you're officially open for business. This is also a great time to run a contest to help get things off to a fast start.

You can do anything you want for a prize when it comes to a contest and what people have to do to be able to enter. When it comes to gaining entry for the contest you can do something such as having people follow you on social media and like and comment on the post. This will be a great way to spread the word about your business. The other thing you could do is have people gain an entry by buying a bag of popcorn from you within the first 48 hours.

This will help to drive sales. As far as the prize is concerned, you could do something such as one free bag of popcorn, a free bag of popcorn every month for a year, a free bag of popcorn, and 50% off of a subsequent purchase, or whatever else you want to do. You could even offer prizes for multiple people by having a first-, second-, and third-place winner. Essentially you can leave the contest open for 48 hours.

Once the 48 hours is up, you can take each entry and put it in a random name generator to determine your winner. The cool thing about contests is that they don't have to be a one-time-only thing. You can run a contest a couple of times throughout the year to help build your following or to help drive some additional sales.

Continue to Post Regularly

The thing about doing a launch is that it is a great way to build momentum. Most people who entered the contest won't have gained anything from you for free, but now they are paying attention. The thing about people's attention spans in the modern age is that they're extremely short.

This is why you need to capitalize on the initial momentum that you build from your initial launch and continue to post quality content on a regular basis. If you're working a full-time job at the moment, posting consistently on social media can be a tough thing to pull off on top of everything else you need to do for your business. However, you have to stay in front of people to get them to remember you.

This is the sad truth but people aren't always thinking about your business like you do. They have their own busy schedule and hectic life going on. You have to get them to stop what they're doing and get them to pay attention long enough to give you a chance.

One way that happens is by showing up time and time again. You'll constantly remind people that they need to give your product a try. That's all it takes because if your popcorn is good people will come back.

Think about this premise in your own life. Not on social media, but it could be anything. Maybe it was an ad you saw. At first, you didn't think much about the product that was being offered. But then you saw the ad time and time again.

Eventually, you end up deciding to buy the product. Imagine though if you only saw the ad once. Then you likely never would've bought in.

The truth is advertisers know that most people aren't going to be ready to buy the first time they're exposed to a product. They will become more open to it as they continue to get exposed to it. So think about this in your case. If you continually post high-quality pictures of your popcorn people will eventually cave.

They'll see your post at the perfect time when they're hungry and that popcorn would sound so good, so they go ahead and buy it. That can't happen though if you're only posting 2-3 times per month. Instead what you need to do is post at least one time per day. So let's go ahead and state the obvious, there are a lot of social media platforms today.

If you have other responsibilities when you're first trying to get your popcorn business off of the ground, such as kids or a job, it's going to be unrealistic to try and post once per day on each platform that exists. Sure that would be the most ideal scenario, but you have to be honest with yourself. This is why it's better for you to bite off what you think you can chew. That might only be one platform, it might be two.

It's better to master one platform and then add in a second platform once you feel comfortable. So start with one platform and work your way up to one post per day and then add in a second platform. It's all about momentum.

Think about what happens to most people who set a New Year's resolution to work out. Most of the time people go from 0 to 100. They likely haven't worked out consistently in years and now they're trying to go to the gym 5 times per week.

If they would instead just go two times and build on that, the habit would be more likely to stick. Instead, people are back to their old ways in a matter of weeks. The same thing will happen to you if you bite off more than you can chew.

You'll eventually slip and stop posting altogether and your business will suffer because of it. You have to remember why you started this business in the first place! Remembering your why will help you push past times when you don't feel like it.

One missed post makes it easier to skip your next post and so on and so forth. So how do you ensure that you don't miss a post? The best way is to plan ahead.

The old phrase, failing to prepare is preparing to fail really is so true. Think about this, if you need to make a post today and you have nothing ready for it, how likely is it going to be that you make the post? Well, it's certainly possible, but if you have a lot of other things going on, it can be easy to push it to the side.

You have to think about what you want to post, create the post, and then actually post it. This can be more work than it sounds like if you don't have a picture ready to go. It can be a lot to get a good photo, which is what you need since you're posting pictures about food.

Your imagery needs to be good enough to entice people to want to buy what you have to offer. The best way to do that is to take your photos well in advance before you need them so that you're not rushed. Creating your posts in batches is the easiest way to stay on top of things and ensure that you don't miss a day of posting.

For example, set aside some time where you do nothing but try and take photos for your posts. This way you can get your lighting and everything else set up so that way you're only switching the type of popcorn that you're trying to grab a photo of. This will save you from having to set everything up just to get one photo. Do the same thing for content ideas.

Set aside time when the only thing you do is come up with ideas. Once you get those creative juices flowing, it will be much easier to keep the ideas flowing. Then once you have a bunch of ideas and photos, it's easy to set aside some time to actually create the posts. Once the posts are complete, you can use software such as Buffer or Hootsuite. This will allow you to go ahead and schedule your post, and then the software will automatically post the post for you when the designated time comes.

So if you schedule a post to go live Thursday at 2:00 pm, the software will take care of it automatically for you. This will allow you to plan accordingly however much you'd like to. I believe it's best to plan out your posts one week in advance but you can do what works best for you and your schedule.

What Could You Possibly Post About When It Comes to Popcorn?

When it comes to content ideas for this business, it can be easy to hit a roadblock. How much unique content could you possibly create for this type of venture? Well, quite a bit as it turns out! There are no boundaries when it comes to popcorn. You don't just have to post about things specific to popcorn.

For instance, it is acceptable to post personal things. You can post about your friends and family, what you're doing for the day, and just general stuff about you and who you are as a person. The thing is you don't want to only post about popcorn because that makes you come across as robotic. Instead, you actually want to build a relationship with your audience.

You want to give them a chance to build some rapport and get to know who you are. This connection will help to build an unshakable bond with your followers, which will help to turn them into lifelong customers. The best way to go about building this connection is through your stories. Stories are different from feed posts because they only last for 24 hours, but they are great for posting short-form content, which is heavily consumed nowadays.

The cool thing is that your story posts don't have to be anything elaborate. You can just create simple posts about things you were already doing anyway. This could be something you made for dinner, a TV show that you're watching, you going on a walk, you going out to eat, or whatever else. There is an endless amount of content you can post about yourself and that doesn't even involve popcorn! When it comes to popcorn-related content, what are some things that you could post about? Well I'm glad you asked because here are a few ideas to help get those creative muscles working:

-interesting facts about popcorn
-the history of popcorn
-your process for making popcorn
-the different flavors of popcorn that you offer
-what makes you different from other popcorn makers
-why you wanted to start a popcorn business
-specials or promotions that you're running
-how you package and ship your product
-asking your audience questions such as what's your favorite snack, when is your favorite time to eat popcorn, which flavor do you like the most, etc

In and of themselves, these posts might not seem like a lot and that's because there really isn't much to them. What matters the most is being able to take an idea and stretch it out across multiple posts. For example, think about your process for making popcorn.

You could show the entire step-by-step process to make popcorn in one video, or you could break it up into chunks and now you've created more content because of it. It's also a good idea to repurpose your content. If you made a post that got a lot of engagement 6 months ago, don't be afraid to repost something similar. The thing is you'll have new followers and old followers who never saw the initial post.

Even people who did see the initial post, they'll be unlikely to remember it and even if they do remember it, what are they going to say, "Hey you already posted this!" As a content creator that can be our worst fear at times, but it doesn't happen. Repurposing content is great because it gives you the opportunity to utilize your best posts over and over again. The name of the game with social media is to consistently show up so that way people are reminded that you are in business and that you exist.

Sell Your Popcorn at Events

You're in the food industry, so when you're selling online, people can't taste your product to see if they like it. You really have to do a good job of producing quality photos to entice people to want to give you a shot. That changes though when you're able to sell your popcorn in person.

By selling in person, people are able to try out your popcorn on the spot, which can instantly get them hooked. This is a great way to help build a loyal customer base. It's harder to build trust online and it's not because you aren't a trustworthy person. It's because people don't know if they'll like it until after they've bought it. When you're in person, you can offer free samples to completely change the game.

If you're selling in person and not offering samples, then you're missing out on some serious potential. So what type of food events should you sell at? Well, it can be anything you can get your hands on! Seriously, popcorn goes well with anything and people get hungry so you can have success anywhere you show up.

I'm talking about flea markets, vendor events, conventions, and even specific food events. By going to these places, you put yourself directly in front of people who wouldn't have found you otherwise. You're still going to have your website working for you 24 hours a day while you're doing this in-person initiative, so you might as well go for it. The question is, how do you make the most of it?

Well for starters as I said, you want to offer samples. The best way to approach this is to have a sign that says free samples. Then when you get a request for a free sample, make it fresh on the spot. This will give the customer the best experience possible, but you may not be able to do this depending on how busy your stand is.

You're going to need to have some popcorn already made for samples as well just in case. The other thing you want to do is make sure that your contact information is easily available. Imagine this scenario, someone stops by at your stand, they get a free sample, and they even buy a bag.

They get home and eventually eat the bag of popcorn and they love it so much. The only problem is, they can't remember the name of your company and now they have no way of buying more. You want to make sure that you have business cards available that you can pass out to people.

Clip them on the bags that you sell or if possible get custom-printed bags so that way your information is on any bag that you sell. It's also important to have business cards ready because there will be people that might not buy on the spot, but may go home and eventually buy. You want to give these people a way to be able to find you again.

The same thing goes for you. You want to capture their information if possible so that you can continue to stay in contact with them and build that relationship. So make sure to grab an email address and have a QR code that people can scan so they can instantly go to your social media page to follow you.

This is going to be the best way to help ensure that you're able to stay in contact with people. If you just go to an event and let people walk away, you're missing out on some serious long-term revenue. Presentation is also important when it comes to enticing people to try out what you have to offer.

Typically you're going to be responsible for providing your own setup, which is actually a good thing. This means you can put in the extra effort to stand apart from the crowd. A couple of simple things will go a long way. The first is getting tablecloths for your fold-out tables. This helps to create a clean aesthetic for your area.

The color doesn't necessarily matter, so go with something like black as it's a good color for a wide variety of situations. The next thing you'll want to do is use risers. These are just little stands but they'll help to add depth to your stand.

So instead of everything just being flat on your table, you can add height to each back row, which will make each of your different flavors stand out. This is a big deal because you'll want to make sure that you bring some interesting and unique flavors with you as well.

If you have some green apple popcorn for example and the color of the popcorn itself is green, you'll want to make sure that it's visible for people to be able to see. It does you no good if you have popcorn that would catch the eye but can't be seen by anyone.

Pay to Be Featured on Food Blogs and Social Media Pages

There's no doubt that people can influence others. And it all comes down to who is saying what. For instance, if one of your friends says that the stock market is going to crash soon, you probably wouldn't believe them if they know nothing about stocks. However, if you had a family member who works in the stock market give you the same advice, you'd be much more likely to believe it.

Even though the advice was the same, it's all about who is saying it. The same premise rings true when it comes to our purchasing decisions. If we see a celebrity that we like using a product, we're more likely to buy because we want to use the same products they do. Now of course paying for a celebrity to endorse your popcorn is going to be way too expensive.

Luckily though in the modern age, we have influencers and bloggers who can help you achieve a good return on your investment by following the same premise as a celebrity endorsement. What you first need to do is research different food blogs and social media pages and then come up with a list of people that you'd like to reach out to. Simply ask if they offer paid promotions or if you'd be able to pay for them to review your popcorn. In some instances, they'll want a sample to see if it's going to be worth their time, which you'll definitely want to do.

Once you start to get some responses, you'll want to compare prices based on how big the following is and what type of engagement they get. In the case of a website, you'll want to ask how many visitors they get per month and how long an average visitor stays on their site. This is key because their traffic might be amazing but people might only stay for 5 seconds before leaving.

If that's the case it doesn't matter how many people are visiting this site, you're not going to be able to get a good return on your investment. The same thing goes for a social media influencer. They might have a ton of followers. But that doesn't matter if nobody is engaging with the content. If someone has a lot of followers but hardly any likes or comments, that's a sign that their followers could be fake and again it will all boil down to you wasting your money.

Make Certain Flavors Available for a Limited Time Only

Do you know what can make something sell better? It's scarcity. If people think they won't be able to get ahold of something, it will make them buy more of it. This is what happened with toilet paper during the pandemic. It was so hard to find which made people want to buy it up any chance they could.

Companies do this all of the time too by making certain items available for a limited time or only during certain seasons. Why not do the same thing with your popcorn? Why not create new flavors that you can tease and launch just like you would do to start your business? Then you can help to drive sales by making the flavor available only for a limited time such as 2 months.

Then when the deadline is approaching you can do a series of posts reminding people that the flavor is about to go away, which will help to create urgency and drive more sales. The cool thing is that you can easily do this 3-4 times per year and as long as it's a unique flavor or one you haven't used in a while, it won't get old. The best part is that there are a ton of different flavor ideas you can utilize so you might as well do this!

Chapter 5: Scaling and Growing Your Business to Unimaginable Heights

As time goes on, your business will grow and grow. Eventually, things will get to a point where you'll have to make changes to continue growing. That can be a scary thing as scaling involves risk, but it is a good thing because it's a sign that you're growing. As of right now, you probably are just trying to get started, but this information will still be good to know for when the time does come. This is why I want to give you some things to think about in regard to scaling so that you are prepared.

What Changes When You Grow

So the first thing you need to ask yourself is if you're ready to grow. The thing is when you're big every decision you make matters far more. One bad decision can set you back way more than when you were small. When you're smaller, you could make a mistake and no one will notice or it can easily be overcome. When you're bigger that same mistake is multiplied. For instance, imagine your website has a slow load time. If you're not getting that many orders, it isn't affecting your sales as greatly as it would be if you're making many sales each and every day.

Ultimately there isn't a definitive way to prepare for this other than to just know that it's really important to be detail-oriented and stay on top of your game. The only thing you can do is be prepared with cash. If you have plenty of cash saved up, this can help you overcome big issues that you run into. When you're small, time is on your side, but things are more urgent when you're bigger.

So I would recommend having at least 6-12 months of operating expenses saved up before you try and move into a physical location or hire an employee. So if you're looking to make a hire, make sure you have money set aside to operate and pay their wages for at least 6 months before you hire anyone. This will help to protect you in case something unexpected pops up which it always does. You don't want to be strapped for cash when let's say your $10,000 popcorn machine needs to be fixed. That's the lifeline of your business and things are quickly going to grind to a halt if you don't have the money to pay for it.

Upgrade Your Equipment

The very first thing you'll want to do when it comes to scaling is going to be upgrading your machine. You'll now be able to afford something more robust and you'll need it to help keep up with your increased demand. A more expensive machine will save you time which is your most valuable asset. If not, get ready to spend your entire day making popcorn.

As far as the size of the machine is concerned, you'll want to think about something that is still reasonable for the space you're operating from. You don't want to get something that's oversized for the place you're working out of. It will likely be the case that you'll need a new machine before you move into a physical location.

So upgrade the machine and then consider reselling it on the secondary market once you need a new machine for the new space that you have. Don't hold yourself back and wait on a new machine until you move out.

Getting a Facility

As you grow you will no longer be able to operate from your own home assuming you're able to do so in the first place. Signing a lease on a new space can be the biggest risk because you're under contract to pay up every single month.

There are also multiple things you have to consider such as what size space you should get. So what should you do? Well, the thing is any mistake during this process can set your business back greatly if you're not careful. The best thing to do is to look for flexible lease options.

Instead of signing a multiple-year lease, look for something that only lasts for 3 months and then is month-to-month afterward. This way you'll be able to pivot if the space isn't a good fit for you. Sure you will pay more per month in doing this, but it is well worth the extra money.

Hire Your First Employee

Hiring your first employee is another big risk you're going to have to take as you start to grow. One bad hire can greatly set you back and depending on the state you live in, it could be a bit of a challenge to let the person go. People steal from companies and take advantage of them, or they're just downright lazy, so you really need to be careful.

You'll definitely want to ensure you do a thorough interview process and even start them off on a probation period to begin just to ensure that they are a good fit for your company. The type of position you'll need to hire first is just general labor. You'll need someone who is able to help you make the popcorn, bag it up, and fulfill orders.

Reach Out to Local Mom and Pop Grocery Stores

Now this is where the fun begins when it comes to scaling. You're now able to do things that you wouldn't otherwise be able to do by yourself or with limited equipment. Part of that fun is trying to get your popcorn into grocery stores. You don't want to try and reach out to big chains because nobody is going to give you the time of day.

But with local shops, you'll have a chance and if they say yes, you'll actually be able to fulfill their orders. All you'll want to do is reach out via phone or email. If you're not having any luck with that, then you can go in person and talk to the manager to get the ball rolling.

Conclusion

Popcorn is delicious and what's even more delicious is getting to make money from it. In order to get things popping off though, you have to be diligent. You have to continually market your business as much as you can to get things off the ground.

Yes, building the inertia in the beginning is the toughest part but once you get going, it's easy to maintain. It will take more work at the start, but that's okay because it will weed out people who aren't that serious about it.

If you don't give up, then you won't have to worry about this happening to you, so stay positive and market harder when you begin to doubt yourself or it feels like you're hitting a wall. That moment will come up multiple times during your entrepreneurial career so don't get phased by it!

www.ingramcontent.com/pod-product-compliance
Lightning Source LLC
Chambersburg PA
CBHW070415230526
45471CB00006B/2818